IN THE BLOOD

Caitlin Press Inc.
3375 Ponderosa Way
Qualicum Beach, BC V9K 2J8
www.caitlin-press.com

Text and cover design by Vici Johnstone

Printed in Canada

Caitlin Press Inc. acknowledges financial support from the Government of Canada and the Canada Council for the Arts, and the Province of British Columbia through the British Columbia Arts Council and the Book Publisher's Tax Credit.

Library and Archives Canada Cataloguing in Publication

In the blood : poems / Alan Hill.

Hill, Alan, 1965- author.

Canadiana 20210314915 | ISBN 9781773860787 (softcover)

LCC PS8615.I46 I5 2022 | DDC C811/.6—dc23

In the Blood

Poems

Alan Hill

Caitlin Press, 2022

Contents

Introduction

This book is a story of brothers and of an illness and the illnesses that came after. I was made as a person, for good and bad, by the experience of growing up with an older brother who received a diagnosis of a mental illness and who spent most of his adult life in institutions.

Poems written directly about that time are interspersed with and framed by work concerning my own later and linked mental health struggles and my move towards a form of recovery.

I would hope that many of the themes touched on in these poems are universal enough to travel across borders and decades—even if the travel documentation may be somewhat muddled and the roads laid out by time not as straight as they could be.

I dedicate this book to my brother Christopher John Hill, who will probably not read it and to whom I will probably never be the brother I could and should be.

—Alan Hill, New Westminster, British Columbia, February 2020

In This Beginning

—which is also the end
—somewhere hot, bland

Maui or Cancun
—vacation lite, factory farmed

a suburbanite's Garden of Eden
just made for me.

Leaving the kids at the pool
I slip away
head down
between the mile-high dunes
that guide me to the beach

towards excited shouts
that call me towards them

where I
find the fishermen
on the ocean's edge
dressed in white lab coats
holding clipboards

a pole
from which my brother hangs

head down in an
ill-fitting sports jacket

an aquatic Mussolini
speared, dragged from the waves:

they have not noticed he is still
alive.

Eating My Own Heart

for Christopher Hill

Overwhelm me brother, obsess me, make me you.

Now—that would be love
and I would need to kill you for that

take an axe to your double bind, see it triple bind
in that silent forest of the beginning of us

the start of humankind, its tight fingered blood
curled in the ear of first light seen by nobody.

That is who we are

we are the sharing of all you have

the needles, tablets, the half-life rooming houses
of the strapped down normality, you are allowed to be

all your death which is nothing but mine
that I cannot live without.

You and I, together

trapped beneath the tree that fell
that could not be heard

that is crushing us with the hardness of love
bedding us on the sharpened points of Eden.

Mother

My mother gifted me a moonstone.

On those nights when my brother made excuses
refused to talk
disappeared into the forest of himself
his quiet desperation

she would wander in the yard
its knee-high grass,
jungle of broken machinery, old washing machines
cookers, abandoned domesticity

hold the stone up, let it net the rays of the moon itself
as she rubbed it into existence
between her finger, thumb
sparked the deities of its light into fire.

What I remember most
was how round that stone was
that it had no beginning, end
it clinched the past, future, together,
in a perfection

I know I still must make that choice, between
silence, defeat, or

what she left me, that I can hold in my palm
close my hand over, form into a circle.

Inheritance

It is this illness of the mind

that has farmed me to the outer acreages of loss

trapped me in a freak show of continuous fresh starts

I have applied an anxiety to my life
with the dedication of a madman.
This is because I am one.

I have baby-gated every thought,
saran-wrapped, sealed all beauty

I must protect myself, not to become myself.

All this insanity to appear sane, stay unnoticed
stay undercover, plan the perfect rebirth that will not come,
the uncontrollable play at being in control

all that time wasted talking to doctors I do not like
about how much I do not like myself

writing out cheques in consultation rooms
studded with Buddhas.

Then I tell myself the lie that I have gained
—illness has made me bigger, better

made me compassionate, class free, an advocate

that there are others
that have gone beyond words, cannot be reached

—but not me, no not me, that will never be me.

Prayer

There he is, my brother who smokes

alone on a winter evening

hardened in silence on the asylum steps

bundled in the unsaid
on the edge of his own life.

his face lit up, shadowed
in innumerable iconographies
quizzical side eyes

his cigarette
being pulled through his lungs
into the reality of this moment
glowing though him in a bruise, redness
a nail head of fire

burnt in the bare arms of the dark.

The Asylum Visit

An inverted Victorian castle build to keep in, not out.

My mother efficiently shuffled me
through identikit corridors
slipped in though security doors onto the ward

past anonymous doctors in crumpled whites
those little worker ants with delusions of grandeur
all clipboard, attitude, smudgy glasses
who never seemed to see you,
moved through you in reptilian slip.

Here was milky cold coffee, a rainbow of medication

the poor, the terminal, the chronic
my older brother, perched silently over a plate of beans

Then the slippers. That was what I wanted to see
Pandas, Sharks, Hippos,
lined in their Largactil parade

Garfields, a Kermit, a Fox head
rooted on curled linoleum. That was for me.

How I envied them, with their exotic footwear

as my mother sat in silence, waited for time to be up
cigarettes burnt down onto carbuncled knuckles
nobody moved.

On the Inside

The grass turns red, my head is on fire
windows break, there is blood, are devils

yet there never is.

I am keeping them from this.
They should be grateful, thank me, love me.
I have saved them. Yet, what do I get
Largactil, the Lord, jigsaw puzzles of
other people's castles, country scenes
that would not exist if not for me
I have eaten the world's violence
keep it down, controlled it.

Then there are those fools, the teachers
social workers, psychiatrists that mocked me,
would not believe

Today I sewed mailbags, swept leaves
watched from behind a pillar
as someone
swapped sex for cigarettes.
I hummed Beethoven, scratched at my wrists,
got bullied for my allowance, for pennies,
kicked for a sandwich.
Ham, mild cheddar, Satan's favourite

Later as I lined up for scrambled egg
I learnt that Jesus had walked off the ward
drowned himself in the canal.

That is not for me, I must eat, keep my strength
If I am to save the world.

Firewatch

It is my brother
that plays with matches in my head

who knows it is all for nothing,

that whatever the intensity of pleasure
the depth of love, that there will be a last time
a return of pain.

It is my brother, who I never talk to
who lives a continent away
who knows my legs are already there

hanging from the fifteenth floor of a city block
waiting for a push, slip

that below me
that there are cops, medics, pacing
who, this time, may not take the catch.

From up here
I can see their cigarettes at night
how they burn with a pure
atom-splitting brightness
with an intensity, then a dimness
as hearts works, lungs pull in, exhale:

Up here this is all I have of them
to prove they are alive, are
watching me.

Older Brothers—France 1963

In this photograph
I am not born yet

My older brothers are
guarding my entrance

scouting out my future ground
in matching t-shirts and shorts
armed in mouths, eyes and hair
that they are holding for me.

Two boys of eight and ten
on a Mediterranean beach

in the certainty of an August heat
that pins their uncertain smiles
into a thicket of steady light

holds them there
jamming clock hands tight
denying time
if only just for them,
just for this moment.

This was before it all

schizophrenia, social workers
the police, the unwilling neighbours
the lives disemboweled
by apathy and accident

couriered away
to unknown destinations
under the ambivalent cosh
of those paid to care.

Whatever they have not been since
they were that day

giving me the heat, light
that I will learn to live by.

Where I Live

Yes, when I bother to notice, allow it
it is perpetually forty years ago, a different
continent

my brother is just home from the hospital

a plastic bag with his belongings
is in the hall,
a slipper with a torn sole
a worn-out toothbrush that has
knifed itself into daylight.

The centre of me is eight, loam,
I have run into the fields at the back of the house
Into the unhurried bud of a plump spring
that has bedded, feeds in the flesh, clay
muscled centre of my existence
on my consequence, perpetual in-consequence.

I am always in that place
in that sliver of unvisited woodland, edge land
that may no longer exist

that is not visible between the highway
wheat fields, the drop to the river's bank.

Leviticus

I sacrificed my youth
gave my body to doctors, psychologists, psychiatrists

dissolved under a cocktail of chemical cosh
the ritual of the weekend binge

drunk the blood, ate the fat of my own accumulation
in the move from city to city, woman to woman.

I bowed to the law of my own anxiety.

I knew it
that if I could hold every fear, think it, imagine it
then I would not be it

every broken window, piss in an alleyway, sex with a stranger
a holiness.

The redemption is the relief
that in a church, chapel, cathedral there is nothing

the possibility of silence.

ECT

They burn away the walls of you
introduce you to calmer places

where you will be at home

although always a tourist
not quite sure
if this is you, how you got here

where you are.

You did not think these thoughts
buy these clothes

they have been brought to you,
given

Yet you will not complain,
you never do

Such is the peace of it
this tourism
that comes so easily, with a flash,
blankness
a mere 120

In the waiting room, before me
an old lady flattened under a stillness
waits her turn
embalmed in milky tea,
balancing a cookie on a saucer edge
listening patiently
to the slow advance of saliva
across her broken dentures.

The Hospital Farm

The pig, as I mucked it out, tried to eat my boots.

All teeth, muscle, pink-skinned eating machine
master of mud, shit.

It could have knocked me down, crunched my bones
although, it did not, would not have.

It is only us humans, that would be stupid enough
to consider that a possibility, so
unsure, insecure we are in our soft casings

unable to wallow in what could make us good
to feel anything but repulsion for our own,
those almost like us, separated by languages, colour.

Over the waist-high wall of the pen
where I could see, the pig could not, the
cowardly bicker of early evening city lights

a thousand needlepoints of sound, sentient, mechanical
the terrifying measurement, weighing, of futures.

The Hospital Dance

On Saturday night, they came in ones and twos from their tiny rooms
for coke and chips, to inch themselves out onto the skin-thin hardwood
shimmy between the flakes of peeled plaster, dropped from uncleanable high ceilings.

They came to dance, move themselves to a squat bomb of antique record player, that
unstably vibrated on a glass-topped table, as

I spun old 45s, donated by concerned relatives, picked up at thrift stores, middles
missing from their jukebox days, from

the days when people once paid to listen, they would have meant something for
people more solid than us,
to those who had edges, boundaries, dreams they could leave behind, had jobs,
shadows that disappeared when they woke.

Well, we had their music now, for a while, a little bit of them as well.

Most of us danced on our own, stretched unfashionable knitwear, yesterday's jeans
become lost in our own moves, disjointed, as we uncoupled our bodies to the beat
worked on being invisible, becoming furniture in dim-lit corners.

That night a girl with smudgy glasses danced with the banisters, a teen with a wispy
beard clapped in a corner, nobody touched:

In fact, nobody ever did touch, not here, where surviving in your own body was
enough knowing it was still there, still moving, however out of step, to your
commands.

The Three Ships

That still dark Christmas morning
mum and I caught between decades
between Woodstock and Watergate

she still young, we still a family

still with a brother whom I knew, who
knew me.

My mother's smile
a swing-bridge, her voice a roadway

with me aged six and she
still in possession of
everything I will ever need to know.

She sang to me
"I saw three ships come sailing in,
come sailing, come sailing in"

a song from before the written word, a
brother of "Greensleeves"

as we sat arm linked to arm
beneath the tree
that cast its armada
of white light
into the dark Atlantic of the lounge.

Before History

My St. Christopher before the fall

before his drinking

the half-cooked buffet of himself

the all you can eat
for cops, physiologists
spiteful neighbours
pitying strangers

before it all
when there was that holiday.

Him carrying me
his little brother on his shoulders
up a stretching vein of mountain track

a delicate line
winding itself airborne
to hook within the gullet
of a hardening fog
to leave us eyeless in a radar of faith
to leap from rock to rock.

I felt it
as he jumped us into oblivion
the smack on the base of his boots
as he found it

this time
only coming to his knees.

The Daily Express

The attic was a model railway.
My brothers, father, took a
third each.

landless
I would watch, as they built stations
created towns, modelled landscape,
populated them with
obedient, clean, people
who did not litter
go on strike

filled fluorescent-green fields
with cows, that never shat
ran away.

When Chris got ill
he painted his third black.

Houses, meadows, engine sheds,
track, all subsumed
under a thick coat of death,
silence.

Still the trains ran on,
such was the denial
the passion for normality, order

Sure, most trains did not stop

passengers
turned their plastic heads away
concentrated hard
on posters on the carriage walls of
cities, beautiful places
they would never get to visit.

Summer Holiday

Mum, dad, and I, made sandcastles.

My brother waded into the ocean
in a jacket, tie
stood there, sang, the water
invited itself to waist level

He was dressed in my father's
hand-me-downs

the kind of clothes old people
will fit the mad in
to make them look normal

a ploy which, of course, never works.

As people stared, pointed, laughed
I was aware how routine this was for us

as by then, we had seen too much
… if there can be too much.

It was a shame he would
ruin those brown nylon slacks

Yet, that may be the cost of it

if your hallucinating brother
who appears to have dropped in
from the 1940s
wants to walk to the end of the ocean

wherever that is.

I pressed on, carefully fitted
a British flag into the top turret

confident things were going to hold.

Disappointment

There can be so much of it
you cannot see the end

It is unmeasurable, dimensionless
impossible to hold.

My father had to see it

how his little boy became a mad man
psychotic, obese, limitless
in his failures
in his lack of insight
in his bringing
of an endless, unremorseful
emptiness.

His good-looking little kid
a monster now, unemployable
unmarriable, unlovable
except to him.

Even then, he was not that sure
his love was strong enough
its spindly, malnourished legs
would hold.

It was a relief when the cat
was crushed by a truck
that as he shovelled up remains
something gave
that at last, he could cry.

Uneasy Rider

My brother only had one job

commuted on his motorbike,
that he would forget to put gas in
or lock, where he had left it

Every journey,
completed a hundred times before
an acceleration
into unknown country.

Sixteen years old.
abandoned by school
to negotiate a virulent uneasiness.

At the garden centre
he would be busy for a while
slowly potted plants
shifted bags of shit
replanted seedlings, then
he would drift.

The manager would discover him
amongst the hothouse blooms

fingers pressed on the glass
as he looked for a hold

as he examined
the silence between leaves.
the budding oddness.

A seeker by mistake, a pilgrim
born though illness
to scatter odd seeds

blank eyes full of everything
that gleaned nothing.

Some forget
where they have left their keys
or wallet

others, who they are.

Vanishing Act

On summer evenings
flagging under the weight of
their own shadows

my brother left home

walked in the hills, the forest

He had no fear

as nothing
could give more death
than what was already within him.

He headed up
through a tangle of darkened cedars
limestone escarpments
beyond the treeline
to disappear into night

Unseen, I often followed him
towards, whatever it was

a cradle of something unknown,
unknowable.

I left a part of myself there
that I can never take back.

Centrefolds

In the fire pit, in the backyard
I burnt my brother's porn.

Sixteen, newly mad
he would come home drunk
with magazines beneath his overcoat.

This was all he ever had for love.

Even then, I think he knew
he would never have a girlfriend,
wife, children
or ever be kissed
not even in pity or drunken mistake.

I would steal the magazines
so I could feel it

the tingled trickle of greatness
the controlled, centred aloneness
that is those first times.

Then it always came, guilt, fear
that sex, madness, were one
the need to burn

to thrust a stick in total dedication
in the destruction of genitals
the fuck-me smiles, spray-on tans,
those legs, open
in moments of perpetual pleasure

my face hot
against the spitting of promiscuous ash
the draining of itself

the act of cleansing
and separating of burning body parts
—the laying out of bones on grass
solid and still
in a proof of sanity.

Night Shopper

That winter, the cops
would bring my brother home at 2 a.m.

complete
with his double-glazed eyes, still then unbroken.

It was usually that they had found him
in front of the stores of bright light
that lined our main street
unsure of where, or who, he was

the octopus of his unmade teenage head
slithering its tentacles out into the road
blocking traffic
wrapping itself around chimney pots
the throats of strangers.

Of course he had been drinking
his pockets hard with porn
—but there was something else—
feeding on him, inside,
not showing, fatting itself for birth

just giving us
the odd movements of fingers in his neck
the imprint
of a boot kicking the inside of an eyeball
the dark wounds
of the communication lines
moving inwards
into places we could not see or comprehend.

On school nights I would lie in bed
and listen to my parents' muffled sobs
—but often as not
between the slow official sentences of tired cops
there was just a silence
of a strident bafflement

a speechless embarrassment
bigger than all of us and beating its chest,
rattling the doors and windows
cupping its body over the house, blocking us out.

Up on the Roof

He was one step away
—hanging one leg as a probe
over the lip of life

momentarily latching his breath
on the rusty guttering
of the tenth-floor rooftop.

A middle-aged man
splayed on an apex of slates,
slipping in flat-soled shoes
on the thin skin of the v-shaped roof.

He could feel the disgrace,
knots of it bursting
in the back of his head

knowing
that he was letting someone down,
although he did not know who,
that he was jumping the queue
between this life and the next

that he owed it to someone
to show patience, wait his turn.

Below him he could see it
the vast machinery of automated life

Firefighters, cops,
the male fraternity
bonded in the spreading of nets
the unstrapping of ladders
the unpacking of bullhorns
and blankets,
the strategic parking
of fat-bodied trucks.

This little army they have made of life,
these ambassadors of being
swarming with a certainty

that just to spite them
made him want to live.

Gold Digger

Mimicking my brother's madness
made me friends

Gave me rebirth
in my schoolboy re-creations
of his strangeness

as I turned
my brother's madness into friendships
capital.

I was the boy who held the key

guarded the door to the exotic
world of the ill
to freak show possibilities.

Even adults were not immune
from what I offered them

I got a laugh
from the lazy-eyed ambulance driver
who was a friend's dad

mum's teacher friend
with the chainsaw tongue

even my parents themselves
with my brother's stillborn life
that they did not know how to dump.

There were those mornings
when I awoke

dripping with guilt

would rub it up against my flesh
watch it as it turned to gold.

Day Patients

Everyday at 8 a.m.
the ambulance came for him,

Really, more a white minibus
with the word ambulance in large letters

so there was no misunderstanding
why so many broken people
were all together in this one place

no worry for the public
that they had not been labelled
were controlled.

My brother would leave them to wait
as the driver, with the face
of a washed banknote,
smacked the horn

I wondered
what it was like to be our neighbours
how lucky, superior, sorry
they must have felt for us.

Then I would be angry at my brother

at what he has done to us
that my mum could not leave for work
I could not finish breakfast
get to school

until he was gone

we heard the sharp slam of doors
the slow acceleration away.

Only Natural

On that Sunday afternoon
when the violence overwhelmed us
my brother's schizophrenia spawned an intensity,
a difference,
too overwhelming for my old-world parents, with
their 'let's keep it normal,' philosophy...
I left the house, sprinted into the fields,
skirted abandoned farmyards, broken tractors, garbage
moved from the edge of our civilization
into wilderness, into forest
up to the mountain's cool lip
into clearing, ferns, ingesting grasses.
I saw the Fox before it saw me
I saw how the scrubs, the trees gave way to it
the air bent, bowed in subservience around its feet.
I smelt the whiff of scat
saw its certainty of risen claw, the
clarity of its bestial self.
How I hated it, wanted to take a rock to its head,
have its pelt.

Silence

Dad would laugh at me...
with my freak show tic
my six-year head full of lead.

I could never hold it steady.

When
your brother has his madness
what is left?

There is no parental love

They have no time to hold you
tell you it will be okay

so busy are they
with the end of everything.

In time, as I reached adulthood
I learnt
to keep myself steady
unsinkable

work in dedicated silence

not ask questions
when I knew
I could not get an answer.

Medical School

The madman would cook until dawn

the back door wide open

as at night
he tried to find a cure for himself

herbs, grass, flowers
sugar, boiled candies, teabags
alchemized
thought soups, potions

My parents
would shout from the top of the stairs

"go to bed Chris—go to bed Chris"

as we drew nearer the dark blank
of the morning's family commitments

work, school, psychiatric clinic

that in our sleeplessness
we already knew we would not meet.

Freedom Fighter

On the locked ward,
his mind has cut itself to chunks.

For safe keeping,
carefully stacked itself under his bed.

He must hide himself
not give himself up to them

with their annihilation though medication

their bibles, bedpans, milky tea, baked beans.

He will survive them all

He is master here in this arena
of the young
that have come to nothing

those victims he has learned to despise

that are to be forever crippled
under that weight
of what those who claim to love them
feel they should have been.

The Throne Room

In Psychiatry, there is that place
with corridors as sure as Camelot

a blood fat grail of padlocked wards
iron bars, fist tight brick.

There is that lake of milky tea,
a raised arm
with a loaded syringe

A moat of processed sausage
and baked beans

the battle smack of knife, fork

enough nylon curtains
bunched in prayer around beds
high barred windows
to stretch cross continent

to surround
those empty moments
stacked like dominoes,
as hard as knuckles

that you bump into
between jigsaw puzzles, Ping-Pong.

There is teenage girl
in her high-backed chair
who is stiller than it is possible to be

hiding beneath a centre parting,
a frozen waterfall of long witchy hair
dropping down
over her body of winter twigs.

There are those skinny young men
who move too fast
with sweaters pulled down
over scars and needle marks

heads steaming with the low fires
of a feudal disappointment.

Recovery

After I left therapy
collected my months of medication

I spent the winter in the basement
studied death rates, infection trends

how those Americans
across the border fight, divide.

There was nothing that could stitch me whole.

No short-term patch, magic pill,
one-word answer, reward.

On that first Monday
the moon, had spread itself
between the open palm of
the neighbour's leafless apple trees

rolled it lazy eye over the simplicity, certainty of
a December frost

threw a blanket of low light over the sill

entered the room
settled itself in certainty over the furniture
anchored, steadied.

Tonight, there would not be darkness.

There will be a street of light

I will sit here, confused, quiet,
read this map of evening with my finger

hold my hands out, to what could be God.

The Applicants

It was not my brother's illness that became us
but all those people that he could have been.

Any time of day or night

a fireman tapped out hellos upon the kitchen windowpanes

bankers whispered through the letterbox

on weekends an accountant
standing to attention by the plum tree

a doctor
looking bored upon the garden wall.

Even the failures of whom we could have been
street sweepers, broken shoe gamblers, poets

would occasionally be at the letterbox
firing resumes, begging notes, staged photographs
photocopies of degrees and diplomas
on to the mat.

Soon every room was full.

We moved to a new house, but the old house followed us.

We took disguises as we moved from something
someone, anything.

My brother dragged corpses from room to room
often still recognizable as him.

The Dream Brothel

Through watching schizophrenia
—that skull-crushing fantasist

I had myself
sucked out of me through my ears

was left with nothing but my mind
glued and nailed backwards

to be ridden in an SS truck, Aktion T4
being driven by me

slaughtering myself
of all my compassion
all weakness
hunting down my own sicknesses
forcing myself
with weak smiles and a loaded revolver
to admit my own fear,
medicalize my every moment.

My belief in my parents was taken
into foster care

my siblings became an embarrassment
to be live beyond

life being all they were not.

My family a defeated City
engrossed in recriminations
jealousy, acts of cowardice
small acts of rescue
gross acts of collaboration
finger pointing

my
flesh and blood jumping from windows
into uninflated life rafts.

Centrepiece

Yes, eventually there came a time when I had to talk
there could be more denial
pretence that I was fine, that I could go on.
To get to that point, took years
cash I did not have
false starts, wrong people in the wrong places.

I had to learn what it is to talk
be led on a journey by a skilled guide

the right guide, the one with the ability to listen
not judge, demand, impose
give me courage to face the spectres, the knives,
cold indifferent mutilations of my fears.

This journey was to have no beginning, end
to know yourself, or not, has no destination
as in a marriage, a friendship, it is the same with yourself

there is always more
Another level, layer, interpretation, story.

We would take each word
examine them, lay them in lines, sort, grade, match
give each one a breath, a body,
make it solid, wood, metal, earth
into form, shapes, patterns,
make pathways, sticks, scythes to beat a clear way.

Learn to read maps, make maps
know a dead-end, a loop, curve through thickets of
ill meaning, understand that on the right journey
nothing is wasted, I will end up there
in the unknown, at the darkened boundary of the
unknowable, then know I am home.

Manhood

He was going to be everyman.
At sixteen he is in a schoolyard. Life
is unfeasibly flared pants, pimples
nuclear oblivion.

Somewhere there is a war to avoid
a future that is mythical, improbable
a blank where there should be a job,
life, love.

At twenty-one he has left home
He is in a pub with work colleagues
beautiful strangers.
He is hungover, wrestles with shadows
doubts, tiredness he cannot define,

what it means to have a brother
that is mentally ill, this flirt with
drugs, drink

the worries that are him now
part of him. The fear of himself,
his limits, possibilities
how they insist on being noticed,
included, give so little back.

There are high windows
that are always there. Other people's
histories, traditions, that impose

There is a pour of spring light
an inhuman greenness, fields, forest
the threat, promise, of unseen cities.

He can see the way it is, the irony,
silliness
that life is cruel, unjust, impossible
yet just goes so, disappointingly quickly.

At thirty he plays soccer in the park, later,
eats a meal with his girlfriend.
Now he knows what love will be for him
safety, friendship,

He cannot risk passion, letting go, in.
Cracks, fissures, bits of him
must be hidden, stitched over.

He knows this defeat, that he can function,
live, exist, until he is better than this.

There is no self-pity, he has it easy.

At forty he is married
walks in Spanish hills, the Alhambra
its scripts, scrolls, marks of faith,
pressed deep into the brick
He is both envious, contemptuous of this
dedication to God.

That evening
his allergies put him in emergency
In the next cubicle a teenage overdose.
She cries, slips in and out of life.
He feels less than he probably should
looks down at his swollen hands, wonders
who they belong to?

At fifty he is in a parking lot
reclines the driver seat
listens to a soccer game, the predictable
back and forth, tribal belonging of
grown men playing sports.
It is his lunchbreak
He has an hour before he is back at his desk
the tedium, security of work.

He has been lucky
he has a wage, identity, however ill-fitting
to go with it

No flares, pimples, no nuclear death

There has been progress
children, pets, home
compromise with love, a form of it.

The First Time

There was nowhere else to go.
After an evening of teenage kissing
It only seemed polite
to end up in her little brother's empty bed
to take our clothes off
look at our slim, wispy-haired bodies,
wonder what was next.

Nothing got hard, nothing done.
What I thought I would feel, I did not.
I felt nothing.
Who I thought I was, the
lust-spiked stud, insatiable lover
had buttoned up, fled

at that moment, was easing up his coat collar,
tugging a cap down over his eyes,
boarding the first bus out of town.

I lay there in the dark
as my nothingness turned into a loneliness
that would not leave, would never leave

although I did not know then
that I would come to live with this,
know it as part of me

It was just that I was young.

In Plastics

Nighttime in the factory.
in the break room, I nursed the little happiness I had
looked out at the trees beyond the sour orange glow
of half empty carpark
for signs of the happiness that should have been.
My foreman, a quiet man, who had once owned a bar
sat in a truce with a lukewarm coffee.
His five years
he had spent in prison for one unlucky, killer, punch
still seemed a lot.
The jaw is soft, fractures, gets pushed into the brain
It is as easy as that.
Behind us, beyond our silence
we could hear big machines, the cogs, conveyor belts
that pushed out plastic into window shapes
unbreakable, invincible.

Wellness

To know where the ice will hold.
Where there is ice. To recognize it for something safe
that will hold my body, cradle my mind.

To know the possible, impossible
except the empty bed, wallet, home
the gaps, pools of dark, where nothing works
no wiring, handrails, no end.

What I have is this, a bed, a cleaner, medication
the occasional social worker
A faith in a force of love, that is beyond me
Does not need me to be perfect, complete
anything but what I am, the
dedication I can offer in this moment

I have accepted that I am broken,
not worse that the others, that tease, look through me.
Not usually.

I have my facts, my lists, my family histories
I know when people were born, the date they died

I cannot know how anyone feels, thinks.
I have milky coffee, television, sunlight in the park
Most of them, the normal, do not even have that
so busy are they with their futures,
that never seem to arrive.

The Brothers

Grief and love are brothers
that live in me, outside of me
come, go, as they please.

Sometimes they play tricks, each
disguised as the other.

That winter, grief, to play with me,
invited me to parties, drink

abandoned me
to long walks home
to follow clean knives of ice, that
angled themselves in moonlight
on telephone wires
winked in mockery

Love, in his disguise
got angry

threw things, accused, expected
more than what was fair, possible

left me torn, stabbed
with my own intentions.

Often, when I got home
I would find them
oblivious to me, holding hands

grief, back to his black clad self
love in florescence, flowered
in embrace with one another
in a whisper of plans, inaudible
entrapments.

It is not that they did not care.
It is that they are family.
They knew that in time
I would see that they were
mine, my duty, responsibility

that family is everything.

Hunting, Fishing

When it rains the sky is blackness over the lake
the trout press into the bank
I am in their current, flow, in how
it, they, travel in my chest.
I plot every movement in my bones.
They are part of me then.

When I shoot ducks, alone on the lake at dusk
there are hundreds, possibly thousands
that rise at once in their fever, in occupation
of their open throats
in call of distress, communication of concern
belonging
in noise beyond time, human possibility,
understanding, the earthly
to raise me from myself, to the edge of space.

I do not kill them out of hate.
It is the way to keep this beauty for myself.

Self Invention

Today my face is not there

just a scarlet red perimeter
mined, wired, guarding empty space

a slowly accumulated collection of un-feelings
deadenings, insults, micro knifings.

I know what I must do.

stitch stories of the past,
imaginings of my future

pull them taut over the empty space
make them meet, connect them

This is how I will come to re-exist
find a life for myself, features
have something to show the world
to tell them I am not yet dead.

Clear-Cut
North of Pemberton

It is harder to kill, destroy, what is known to you.
That is the theory. That when you have a map of the sap
a trail of rain across bark, pathways, pointers
in front of you, that lead into the forest, a darker silence
that there may be answers, rest.

If I had the patience, the nerve, which I do not
ditched science, the human,

then I could understand depth, width, twist of trunk
how each ring layer marks a triumph over death
scatter of leaves on the forest floor, are the
patterns, precision, that mark our lives

how to the seasons, our hands, mouths, open, close
at the insistence of the wind
birds circle in flightpaths, spell it out, compass us in
compel us to live.

Delivery by Foot

I run beyond the last house lights
people
between the prison site,
red, green Christmas lights
on to the loose gravel, dog leg track
into the valley bottom

There is just enough moon to guide me

enough fear, tinged with relief
to pull me on, forward in the dark

I know that I am lucky to have them

the people in my life, that love me

a practical, loving, wife, good kids
that they are what saves me,
keeps me intact

There are those moments
when I need to be alone

breathe out the confusion, fear,

know
what it is like to leave myself behind
leave the wallet, keys, licences of myself
my official being

know nothing but my breath, the pump
of my blood
that there is a measure of control
over what can never be controlled.

Nighttime in the Ravine

Down I go, into the blue, lucid ice
labyrinth of liberty in winter light
ghost lines, desire lines,
the uncurling crozier of being
in footfall song lines, unreadable,
the press of my boots
over the unknown meteor of each moment

Above me, a crow's lyric crackle

in my hand
the world in the perfection of a fallen egg

behind me there are
blind roads, shallow ways
a suburbia, an apocalypse, lockdown,

in front are possibilities

the stories in each rock
in the move of treetop, in late day light

in the coyotes, their collection of votaries
as they cross the border between being
otherness

that pull me
in the homeward channel of the path
into the dissolve of solid geography
the rules of resonance
misfiring medication
rise of the clear grey water of nothingness
everything

in the death of sunlight
in this unknown knowledge, freedom
this pathway in the dark, where I must go

where my mind cannot take itself
cannot find a reason, logic,
without each step, that is only mine to tread
one foot at a time, down into meaning.

The Coyotes in the Ravine

A rare place, not yet Astroturf
where at twilight,
there are the Coyotes.

One, two, at distance,
that look at me, slip away
transmute into undergrowth
aware
I am dangerous, not trustable.

I admire them for that
how well they know me
recognize my docility
neutered, bloodless humanity

that it is deadly.

I have bastardized myself
to secure a roof, acceptance
food, love

I should admit what I know
that without wildness
there is no order,
without darkness, filth, no purity

without the misshapen, broken,
incalculable
there is no proportion, shape

without Coyotes in the ravine,
I have nothing.

The Human in the Ravine

He will never be so alien, apart, pointless
as he is here in this ravine, where
he brings nothing to the Coyotes, Raccoons
but a whiff of his dubious deodorant
additive, scrabbled, hormones, tint of piss, shit

in his unclassified cocktail of human uniqueness
inherent danger, unknown consequence, instability

a sickly tapestry of shade, light, unsure scents
unstable possibilities,

pathways of himself
that lead nowhere known
with no promises of food, shelter

Tonight, he sees it, here in this silence, aloneness,

he is poseur, impostor, ball of unravelled thoughts
rolled with no reason into the evening.

an inconsequential hem of cornea thin colour
that clings on the edge of a blanket of darkness

this sliver of wilderness, between the old penitentiary
the mental hospital.

Lost land, forgotten, too

geographically illogical to be of use
where every animal has it place, function,
except him.

Here, he can take every freedom that he needs
give so little in return.

Although he knows it
the danger of this freedom, with its lack of distraction

in which he may come to realise
he has wasted his life
the jobs, friendships, commitments, mean nothing

that he has failed to be what he can be, love
whom or what he should have loved.

This, the risk he must take
if there is to be more, a future

Above, on the ridge, suburbia, the
stale wink of big screen TVs, lights in bathrooms,
bedrooms
the signals of his neighbours, people like him
as they ready for bed, tomorrow's workday.

He is lost here, does not have a role, his
own link in the food chain, the mutual aid of
becoming something's breakfast.

What he has is chain of memory,
part of the thoughts, feeling of his father
a little less of his father's father, then
further back into darkness
the remote physicality of history
drawn real in his own facial features

The rich have philosophy, ideas, edge land,
inner, outer space bought through money
adrenaline, sex.

He has the ravine, its animals that step around him
keep themselves apart from him, as they must
to survive all his frustrated ambition to exist.

Sanity

He become sane
—starting
as someone else
who used his ears
took his sight for their own.

There was no him
he was no agent to himself

could not agree
that he was real,
apart, whole
not animal or machine

There was nothing true,
worthwhile, just his

yet that itself
become continuous

a position in space, in time
a body with an inside
and an out

a movement
from one place to another

a pathway began at birth
and ending at death

a chance for forgetting
an introduction to the self.

Epilogue

In the end after the drugs, incarceration
enforced lovelessness, poverty

it was worth it all.

He knows it now, how he will always be strange
different
not one of them, perhaps, not really
even part of his own family.

He has his room, TV, La-Z-Boy, fridge
fish suppers, coach trips with the social group, bingo
Catholic church one day, Protestant the next
in the open shop of Jesus, his friendly people.

He has his childhood memories
from before this thing
his brother, sisters as they were
stored, untouchable, still real.

all the images, ideas, things the
doctors, psychiatrists could never reach

He is settled now, calmer, happy to be still
to sort, look deeper, find a truce

be all that is there, peaceful, alive, beneath
the disguise of his broken body
ill-fitting skin.

Acknowledgements

Poems in this collection have appeared in *The Antigonish Review, Beatific, Black Sunflowers, Poetry is Dead, The Denver Review, The Sextant Review, Very Much Alive: Stories of Resilience (The Selkie, 2021)* and *Wingless Dreamer*.

I would also like to acknowledge the help and support of my colleagues in the writing community, including Joanne Arnott, Miranda Pearson, Janet Kvammen, Candice James, Rachel Rose and many others.

Last, but not least, I would like to thank Vici Johnstone, Sarah Corsie And Malaika Aleba at Caitlin Press for believing in this project and for their ongoing support.

AUTHOR PHOTO BY MICHELLE GOLDBERG

About the Author

Alan Hill was born in the UK and immigrated to Canada in 2005 after meeting his wife while working in Botswana. He is the former Poet Laureate of the City of New Westminster, BC (2017-2020), former president of the Royal City Literary Arts Society (RCLAS), and was the editor and curator of *A Poetry of Place: Journeys Across New Westminster*, published in partnership with New Westminster Arts Services. His writing has been published internationally and his poetry has appeared in *Event*, *CV2*, *Canadian Literature*, *The Antigonish Review*, *subTerrain*, *Poetry is Dead*, among others. He works in the field of community development and immigrant settlement and lives in New Westminster, BC.

In the Blood is typeset in Arno Pro. Designed by Robert Slimbach, Arno was crafted in the tradition of early Venetian and Aldine book types. Named after the river that runs through Florence, the center of the Italian Renaissance, Arno draws on the warmth and readability of early humanist types of the 15th and 16th centuries.

&